Bouncing Back

Your Mental and Emotional Resilience in the 'New Normal' and Beyond

by

H Michelle Johnson

First Printed in United Kingdom 2021

Published by Conscious Dreams Publishing
www.consciousdreamspublishing.com

Edited by Lee Dickinson

Typeset by Oksana Kosovan

ISBN: 978-1-913674-60-1

DEDICATION

To my maternal aunt, Antoinette Guerra.

Thanks for always being the head cheerleader in my 'village'.

PRAISE FOR BOUNCING BACK

"Your book is OUTSTANDING!!!! It is powerful, shows vulnerability, strength, and a manifestation of wisdom. The tips are awesome. I'm totally impressed and want my students and colleagues to read this when it's published."

~Tiffani Michelle Mapp,
Psychology and Mental Health Services
Professor and School Counsellor, College of
Central Texas.

"Bouncing Back is a necessary book. We have been facing a mental health pandemic for quite some time now. An honest and vulnerable approach is needed to reach the public in the most gentle yet practical way. Bouncing Back does exactly that. Through journeying with the author, the reader explores highs and lows of their own processes, enabling them to take targeted action. I strongly recommend this book to both the public and to practitioners. At the time when integrative approaches are needed, this will allow them to bridge the gap between what's human and what's clinical."

~Joanna Kukla,
Health and Well-being Coach, London.

"This book is brilliant and will help so many."

MESSAGE FROM THE AUTHOR

Hi, I'm H Michelle Johnson. Thank you for reading my book. I'm an author, broadcaster, coach and business person. The major part of my working life has been as an adult nurse (18 years) and then a Communications and Engagement Specialist (approximately ten years) in the National Health Service in the United Kingdom.

I was a Clinical Nurse Specialist and Research Sister in the field of cancer genetics in my last nursing role. For ten years I counselled and supported people in their journey to reduce their risk of gynaecological, breast and bowel cancers and complicated bereavement experiences.

It was a role to which I was dedicated, and very passionate about. During this period of my career, I began to experience anxiety and low moods. As these symptoms persisted over several months, I decided to see a doctor and was told that depression was the cause. That came as a genuine shock. For eighteen months I remained in denial about it, sinking further and further, until I had no choice but to face it. In doing so, I discovered so much that empowered me to bounce back. I learned key strategies for self-care, which have enabled and sustained my recovery from that period of heightened anxiety and low moods fifteen years ago.

These self-care strategies have created high levels of resilience: that ability to bounce back from adversity which is so critical to well-being.

Whatever your situation – whether you're experiencing 'the blues', you're worried about the future or at a place where you recognise the need to be more proactive about your own well-being (self-care) – there is a lot in this book you can take away to meet your needs. None of us are immune to life's setbacks, but we can each support our personal well-being by actively building resilience, so that we can bounce back from adversity.

In this book I share with you bits of my story, and how I recovered, along with strategies I still use to self-care. Using these strategies over the years has created high levels of resilience. They empowered me to take back control of my well-being and create a life of meaning and impact. I am living a productive, richer, more joyful and fulfilled life as a result.

Focusing on the fulfilment of my purpose, dreams and goals has been a powerful energiser throughout my journey. Through talks, workshops and one-to-one coaching, I have helped others to transform their mindset, using many of the strategies in this book. My first book, *Do Great Exploits, Saying Yes To Your Dreams When It Is Easier To Say No*, won the Wise Women International Awards Book of the Year Prize in 2021. Since its publication, I have received invitations to give TV and radio interviews, speak at numerous events, including in the United States, Caribbean and UK, being hosted by Unison, the Royal College of Nurses, Central Texas College, University of Coventry, Middlesex University, Nurses Association of Jamaica UK, The Jason Roberts Foundation, to name a few.

I had the honour of being nominated to speak to the United Nations, Sustainability Development Goal 11: Sustainable Cities and Communities, as part of the 75th Anniversary of the UN. I hosted radio talk shows including The Women 101 Show (Prayz.In Radio), Need 2 Know (Flava Radio), The Great Xploits Show (Slam Radio UK) and Chatback (Radiolere). During lockdown, I created the Great Exploits Features Series (Instagram live), speaking with innovators about resilience and effectiveness in challenging times. I haven't listed these activities to impress anyone, but to highlight that adversity absolutely does not have to be the end of you. It is possible to bounce back, no matter what life throws at you, and regardless of how difficult, unfair or challenging it is.

In retrospect, the diagnosis of depression seemed to give me a profound drive to discover my purpose in life, an appreciation of time's value, plus a resolve to maximise my life meaningfully. It led me to take stock of my life, reconnect with myself on a deep level, think about what I really wanted, and then set about achieving it. It turned out to be a great propeller.

Resilience: the ability to bounce back from adversity

Without it, I may well have continued drifting along, going wherever life's currents took me, while always dreaming of something more. Maybe it's pride but, when faced with adversity, I do not surrender and go quietly into the night. Fifteen years ago, and still young, ambitious and hungry to do something with my life, I was outraged and exasperated when confronted with depression. Being armed with knowledge of what my enemy was, I decided I was going to fight to win. Adversity can either be a destroyer or a game changer in our lives – it is up to us to decide which it will be. Adversity is like Judas – a 'frenemy', as the young people say. It manifests as a person, a circumstance or an event that ushers you into a season of hardship and pain.

The COVID pandemic ushered many people into unspeakable hardship, loss and pain. But regardless of how difficult your situation, I am of the view that as long as you still have breath, there is still hope for you. The starting point is believing. You have the power to decide how you cope with life's many diverse trials. You have the power to define what winning looks like in the battles you face. You have the power to create that win. I take the example of Christ in this. It was his 'frenemy' Judas who facilitated Christ's ultimate win. Judas betrayed him, got him arrested, setting off a chain of events that not only led to Christ's execution, but his rising from the dead – saving anyone who believes, in the process. When life knocks you down, rise again and bounce back. Let adversity be the wind beneath your wings, lifting you to new heights of progress and achievement. Make Judas regret he ever laid his beady little eyes on you! That's the wonderful role that adversity can play in our lives if we approach it with the right mindset. What's happened to you in the past months or years that you've struggled to bounce back from? There is something in this book that can help you to do so, going forward.

FOREWORD

Who would have thought that a global pandemic would change the ways we connect socially? 2020 has proved a game-changing year for me as a Psychology and Mental Health Services Professor, School Counsellor and Life Coach. One such game changer was meeting H Michelle Johnson; a woman I consider to be phenomenal and inspirational.

We met when I was a guest on her talk show, 'Chat Back', which she co-hosts with our mutual friend, Chef/Author Lyndon Wissart. During our conversation, there was an instant, organic connection between us as if I had known her for years. We quickly developed our new-found friendship and I was honoured when she sent me her autographed book, *Do Great Exploits*. Impressed with her vast knowledge, wisdom, charm, and authenticity, I invited her as a guest speaker to talk to my psychology students at Central Texas College in Killeen, TX, on the themes in her first book, and be a voice of inspiration to them on life purpose.

In her presentation, Michelle shared about her experience with depression during her career as a specialist nurse and researcher. I am thankful she shared her story, because sometimes there is stigma when discussing mental health, especially in minority communities. This beautiful work, *Bouncing Back*, is profoundly written, and infused with deep insight on this important topic. Michelle's candid sharing of her experiences of this condition, plus the strategies she's used to build resilience, are scholarly yet written in a style that is appealing. *Bouncing Back* will inspire you during the sunshine and the rain as you learn to weather the storm through self-awareness, embracing change, being mindful of your mental and physical wellness, create a mindset of resilience, and implement strategies to support wellness needs – mind, body, and soul. I am grateful for this book and will be sharing it with my college students, colleagues, creatives, and friends as we support our mental and physical health needs, especially during this pandemic. Also, I will be using this resource as a supplement in my psychology and mental health services curriculum. God bless, and may *Bouncing Back* be a resource and blessing for your self-care needs.

Respectfully,

Professor Tiffani Michelle Mapp,
M.CJ, CSC, LCDC-I

PREFACE

Following the ruthless slaying of George Floyd, I was contacted by many people, both younger and older, seeking help to cope with all that was unfolding. This terrible incident occurred against the backdrop of a life-threatening pandemic that had forced us into the unusual circumstance of a 'lockdown'. It was a recipe for heightened levels of fear, worry, bewilderment, anger, even anguish and depressed feelings. In response to being contacted, I hosted an online event, *Pearls: an ongoing conversation with black women on their infinite worth*. I felt that the response shouldn't just be yet another conversation about the injustice of racism. I wanted to create the opportunity to refocus on the foundations of well-being and resilience and to restore a sense of equilibrium, that would enable them to bounce back with strength, wisdom and resolve.

I'm under no illusion that the road ahead for the world at large and, therefore, for us as communities and individuals, is both tough and uncertain. Key skills related to a healthy mindset, self-care and resilience will be required to help us navigate through the uncertain times with greater effectiveness. I'm not a doomsayer or even a pessimist. I hold on to optimism while never losing sight of reality. I find this helps me to be pragmatic. It helps me prepare. It helps me overcome, carry on, even win in life. And isn't that what we all want? That no matter what might be unfolding or what we might be facing, we will not be hopelessly defeated, but instead be resilient – more than able to get back up and move on to better things?

This is what my hope is for you in the 'new normal' and in life as a whole, now and in the future. The COVID-19 pandemic and various lockdowns produced an increase in people feeling low, anxious, worried, fearful, isolated and lonely. Millions of people have experienced loss of jobs and income. The outbreak caused major disruptions to our daily lives. Millions have suffered bereavement of loved ones. For some, the bereavement process is complicated by the impact of restrictions, which separated them from loved ones in the days running up to their deaths. The authorities' management of the pandemic introduced a new way of life, which is being commonly referred to as the 'new normal'. It is characterised by

an epic reworking of the way we conduct the business of daily life: altering our working arrangements, affecting our movement and travel, requiring that we wear facial masks, redirecting the methods for our communications, reshaping (and disrupting) the way our children receive their education, while changing a host of other aspects of ordinary life. It's as though we are being forced to use the civil freedoms that we took for granted – at least in the Western world, but which now feel extremely precious to us – as bargaining chips in a game of roulette, against an indiscriminate and sinister opponent named COVID-19.

The full emotional and psycho-social impact of these intrusive lifestyle changes being thrust upon us have yet to be measured. In many cases these impacts will also need to be studied in light of economic catastrophe in the business sector, with its knock-on financial adversity being visited upon many families and individuals. Prior to the pandemic, the social structures in which we operated had already begun eroding the integrity of our human connections. Technology played no mean role in the impairment of some of those connections. Remember the endless memes of people sitting at dinner tables but focusing on their phones instead of interacting with each other? What about the self-checkout machines that have all but completely obliterated opportunities for pleasantries to be exchanged with the checkout ladies (or gents) in our local supermarkets? What about evenings in households where Dad would be watching TV, while Mom surfed the internet and the kids were somewhere in the house on their own, fixated on some video game, or texting friends and barely catching sight of each other all evening, let alone having meaningful conversations? Now, in the UK, to access your family doctor you may have to fill in a form and do an 'e-consult' online or phone when you're not feeling well. We may well start looking back on those days with nostalgia, recalling them as the 'the good old days'. With the shift of our activity and communication from being largely face to face, to digital, I can't help but think the erosion of that vital sense of connection with others is bound to increase.

This issue of connectedness is important to mental and emotional health and well-being. Without those connections, thriving becomes difficult. Resilience – the ability to bounce back from adverse times – requires healthy connections. None of us thrives in isolation. We need friendships, family, healthy working relationships. We were created to be in relationship with other people. One of the symptoms I recall when I was anxious and low was feeling detached – even in a room filled with people. In the period when it went untreated, I seemed to lose touch with how to make and maintain those connections. This led to isolation and loneliness. I'm no longer acutely anxious or low, but I've not forgotten what an awful and frightening experience it was.

If you are losing connections with people, you are not alone. Loneliness is one of the plagues of modern life. The good news is that it's not incurable. With a little effort, and patience, it is possible to bounce back to establishing social connections that are good for the soul.

Self-awareness plays an important role in addressing this. I made some key decisions, which may seem quite basic or obvious now, but in my mid-thirties, they had the weight of real importance to my long-term health and my future.

I decided that I wanted a good life, and to enjoy living. I decided my good health was worth fighting for. I resolved to do the work needed to achieve this. I had to consciously choose to open up again and allow those connections to occur on a deep level.

Habitually wearing a brave 'I'm OK' mask when you feel the opposite might protect you, but it also keeps people out. Pretending we're OK when we're not is one of the many maladies of Western culture. We put on emotional masks every day so as not to 'worry others' or appear vulnerable. Behind those masks, some people languish in self-imposed prisons of fear, worry, anxiety, or pain, of all descriptions. They become less connected, being caught up in this cycle.

The facial masks, the closed doors, the social distancing mandated in the pandemic, creates additional barriers to inter-human connectedness. They present physical and geographical obstacles to relationships while building walls of isolation around the more vulnerable among us. And so the 'new normal' requires that we be more intentional about fostering our connectedness to others in order to safeguard our emotional and mental well-being. Whether you're feeling the 'blues', you're anxious, worried or experiencing the more persistent symptoms associated with depression, the principles and strategies outlined in this book can help. Over the years, they've made the world of difference to me, and that's why I share them with my clients.

A note about the condition referred to as depression:

Depression is a mood disorder resulting from biochemical changes in the brain. These biochemicals, or neurotransmitters, give us feel-good, happy sensations, regulating our moods. It is thought that changes in their levels give rise to a range of persistent symptoms such as apathy, decreased motivation or sadness, to name a few.

If you're feeling 'blue' or low in mood, it doesn't necessarily mean you have depression. It is possible to feel depressed without having depression as a health condition. Due to the ups and downs of life, our moods change like the tides of the sea. However, if you notice any of the symptoms I've mentioned, or others, which persist for weeks or months, it may be worth having a chat with your doctor.

I believe the strategies shared in *Bouncing Back* can lift the spirits of anyone feeling low, and strengthen them. Intentionally applying them will go a long way to building and maintaining your resilience in changing and uncertain times.

You only get one shot at life. Fight for the best life you can live!
Know that you are worth fighting for – whatever your circumstance.

We must now adjust to the changes ushered in by this new era in which we collectively find ourselves. Effective adjustment requires we become more intentional about managing our emotional responses, and caring for our emotional and mental health and well-being through building personal resilience.

CONTENTS

1. FIND YOUR RAY OF HOPE AND GRASP IT

Whatever you may be experiencing in life right now that is triggering anxiety, low mood or sapping your resilience, believe me when I say, there is hope. That hope will take on a different form for each person. Hope is something we look forward to with expectation and is very important to our psychological well-being. Hope is supposed to motivate us, fill us with passion, give us drive. Without it, life is flat and unsavoury – hopeless. Hope gives life meaning in the best of times. In difficult times, hope becomes a lifeline that enables us to find our way through adverse circumstances.

As individuals, when in adversity, we must find our own personal ray of hope. If you've lost your job, focus on the hope of finding another. If you've lost your business because customers couldn't come through your doors, focus on opportunities for doing business in a different way. If you're experiencing difficulty in a relationship, focus on finding healthy ways to resolve it. The point is to not get stuck by focusing on the problem; to not slip into a mindset of defeat or that it is all over for you. Finding your ray of hope and grasping it, i.e., focusing on it, will enable your ability to bounce back.

Some problems are stubborn and take time to resolve. But they can be resolved. It may be that you have to change your definition of 'resolved'. It might be that you have to let some things go because that's the only way of resolving them. It might mean that you have to adjust your expectation. This can take a lot of pressure off psychologically, thereby reducing feelings of frustration, anxiety or hopelessness. This approach can be really helpful when you're facing something that cannot be changed. This worked well for me when I was still struggling with low mood. I found my hope when I adjusted my expectation about depression.

I once hoped that I would be cured, or healed of the condition. Living with that hope left me quite frustrated. That frustration fuelled hopelessness and was eroding my resilience. I decided then to change my expectation, so that I could remain in a place of hope within the reality of my situation. Persisting in unrealistic expectations can negatively affect your emotional and mental resilience because the expectation cannot be met and results in disappointment and frustration. If this cycle persists, your resilience will diminish over time. My ray of hope changed from finding a miracle cure, to enjoying a productive and fulfilling life through skilful management of symptoms. That hope has been realised.

Finding your ray of hope in the midst of your personal situation can be a lifeline.

You can bloom in any circumstance.

In retrospect it was a pivotal period for me. Far from feeling powerless, accepting this reality empowered me. I could now look up and determine the way forward. My way forward was to learn new skills, renew my commitment to my dreams, instead of being overcome by an adversity.

I adjusted my expectation so that I could remain in a place of hope within the reality of my life

What is your hope? There are many reasons to have hope. If you have children, you may identify the many hopes you have for each of them, and focus on getting there. I've heard many stories from people facing challenges brought on by the pandemic. A father lost his job. His daughter is a university student. He shared how sad he felt about not being able to support her as he had been doing. He was applying for work in his industry but being turned away. The daughter also spoke about not being able to find any part-time work in shops or restaurants. The family were facing the possibility of having to access the social benefits system for the first time in their lives. The pandemic has posed a threat not only to health but also to people's lifestyles – even their value systems, as per the example above. He was a man who had never thought he would ever face relying on help from the state to pay his bills or feed his family. The prospect is a blow to his identity as the provider for his children. It was evident that he wasn't happy about being in that position, personally.

With millions unemployed, people find themselves forced into unknown territory; their socio-economic status dramatically altered, with all the psychological effects this would inevitably have on them. Yet this father, who was knocking on doors but being turned away, remained fairly buoyant. He was concerned, but grasped a ray of hope by looking at options for retraining and redirecting his employment efforts elsewhere, or possibly becoming self-employed. He was convinced that, eventually, things would work out. His resilience struck me. The situation was tough and there was some work to do, but there was a glimmer of light at the end of the tunnel, and he was resolved to moving toward it. His hope was that he would find work and continue providing for his family, even if it meant retraining and doing something different. This is how hope translates into purpose and gives us the resilience to

bounce. We can choose to invest our energies each day to realise that purpose.

Financial trouble is one of the biggest causes of worry and unhappiness in people's lives, next to relationships. The pandemic has also blown the top off long-standing inequities existing in our society, showing a much greater impact and poorer outcomes for people who are Black, Asian or other Minority Ethnic backgrounds. People living in more deprived areas were also harder hit than the more affluent.

Systemic inequality is a much wider issue than COVID.

It's critical to acknowledge this important driver of undesirable outcomes in any discourse on building resilience and boosting mood because, by its very nature, systemic inequality inflicts weighty, potentially life-limiting psychological, social and emotional impacts on individuals and families, while destabilising communities, cities, even countries. Inseparable to that is racism, which of itself extracts a psychological and emotional toll on those it's dealt to and, I dare say, it must take its toll on those who deal it out too. Hatred towards others has an essentially deleterious effect on the hater. In my opinion, deprivation and racism are among the biggest public health issues of our time.

Finding your ray of hope may appear a monumental challenge in the times in which we find ourselves. But it isn't. Hope can be found in a purpose of your own choosing. That's powerful. In a world where so much seems to be decided for us, there is still opportunity to decide for oneself how you will move forward from where you are.

Finding hope builds resilience to keep bouncing and moving forward until your situation changes. Hope and resilience are two sides of a coin. Progress made to realise the hope you carry brings a sense of achievement and satisfaction, giving the impetus to carry on.

The psychological, emotional, spiritual, even physical benefits of finding hope, cannot be exaggerated. Hope inspires purpose. It inspires action. It changes behaviours for the better. Acting on your hopes or aspirations draws you further away from feelings of powerlessness. Simply taking action in line with what you hope for gets you caught up in meaningful activity, which stimulates and engages the best parts of your mind and capacities. Hope is a cornerstone of resilience.

2. DON'T IGNORE THE ISSUE

When I was diagnosed, I refused to accept it, choosing to go into denial. I swept it firmly under the carpet. This didn't make it go away: it delayed me getting better and thrust me into eighteen months of hard struggle.

In my experience, going into denial about a thing doesn't help. Trying to pretend something isn't real or that it's not happening never really works in your favour. Denial may provide you with some comfort, but it's only temporary. Sooner or later, whatever you're avoiding is going to catch up with you.

This is particularly true when it comes to your health. Over time, you're also likely to find yourself worse off for it than if you had dealt with it earlier.

Like it or not, the 'new normal' is here and may carry on for an in indeterminate amount of time – even with the roll out of vaccines. The efficacy of the vaccines that were first available may change in response to new mutations of the virus. Additionally, these first vaccines seemed to come with some notable limitations. I'm not a scientist. I don't confess to understand the complexities of 'herd immunity', or to what extent achieving this for coronavirus will allow pre-pandemic life, as we knew it, to resume. I think it might be safe to say the 'new normal' will be around for some time, to varying degrees. Avoidance of that fact won't make it go away. But facing the reality, working out what it might mean for you, can enable you to be flexible, and respond more effectively to any changes it creates for you personally. It offers the opportunity for you to plan, prepare and act in your best interest, whether for your health, your finances or your family. In so doing, you will be more resilient when it comes to coping with it.

If you are unsure about taking the vaccine, don't ignore the issue. Go and do your own research – but use only reputable sources that provide sound evidence. Talk with people who have taken it if you can.

Denial is a bit different to saying, 'I'm not ready to deal with this situation.' This stance is at least an acknowledgement of the situation, and a recognition that it needs to be addressed. At the same time, you should be cautious with this approach, as procrastination can only make some situations worse. Putting off dealing with important issues, drains energy. The longer you use avoidance, the more likely it will be to affect how you feel emotionally and psychologically, making bouncing back all the more challenging.

This is the case for the 'little' things we need to get done too: household chores, calling that utilities company, running errands, decluttering, paying your bills and so on. These aren't exciting activities and so we naturally want to avoid them. But making a 'to do' list of the 'boring' things and then crossing items off the list as you complete them, can be! Another strategy is to give yourself a time limit. An hour to declutter a wardrobe for example, then set about racing against the clock; simple but effective hacks to stop avoiding the unpleasant but necessary tasks. When we recognise that we have accomplished a task or project, the brain releases a chemical, a neurotransmitter, called dopamine. Dopamine generates positive feelings of satisfaction, happiness and accomplishment. Getting things done can boost your mood and give you the impetus to get even more done. Facing what you have to do and getting it done will leave you in a much lighter mood.

3. TAKE OWNERSHIP, HAVE A PLAN

Life can positively change, blossom and bloom when we embrace the fact that no one else is responsible for making us happy but ourselves. Our well-being and circumstances are also largely down to us. It's a powerful revelation, yet many haven't had it. Knowing this will liberate you from so much angst, frustration and stress. Each of us has more control over our joy, peace, progress and ability to achieve than we know.

For several years I worked on a ward where I felt excluded, not part of the 'family'. I knew they had a level of regard for me, but it was clear that I was not 'one of them' and it was because of racial differences.

I was under great pressure to be less myself, and more like the dominant group. This experience of mine fits with an emerging concept, which was originally used in linguistics, called 'code-switching'. At the time I was unaware that that was what was happening to me. What I did know was that I would be ignored if I spoke a certain way, marginalised if I brought a view that was different to that which was commonly held, intimidated if I dared make any attempts to lead, and often treated as though I was invisible. These and other micro-aggressions had a wearying effect on me.

'Code-switching' refers to language and behaviours – in particular where people feel the need to adapt themselves to suit environments where the norms or rules are different to what they know.

We all 'code-switch' depending on who we're speaking to, or where we are. For instance, the way we speak or behave in the company of close friends is different to when we're in a work meeting – that is acceptable. However, recent studies by researchers are revealing that people of colour feel the need to 'code-switch' in far more situations than their white counterparts; the reason being that the rules in social situations tend to be framed by white people's experiences. In other words, 'white' ways of behaving become the standard to which others must adjust their own behaviours. A specific example might be the way we express ourselves. People of colour may feel under pressure to change their accent, or 'talk white', in an attempt to avoid being 'othered'.

Stress occurs in these situations, which over time can adversely affect mental and emotional well-being and potentially break down resilience.

As time moved on, I found another job at a higher grade, with more leadership responsibility. I handed in my resignation. What then ensued became one of the most important lessons about people I've ever learned. Staff had got together and collected several hundred pounds, which they gave to me in vouchers as a leaving gift. The same colleagues who at one point or another had been rude, disrespectful, at times downright mean, or treated me unfairly, came to tell me personally they were sad to see me go. I shouldn't forget them. I should come back and visit, etc. It was incredible hearing all that.

Racism is a peculiar disease – who can understand it?

I've used those painful micro-aggressions to propel me forward. Difficult experiences have worked out for me in the end, as they motivated me to move higher and higher. I don't get stuck anywhere. I climb. Approximately twelve years later, it so happened that I was chairing a breakout session at a national nursing conference. Two colleagues from those days were in the audience. They'd been brought along by the Director of Nursing at the hospital. It was good to see them after so much time; I was keen to catch up with them on some of the staff who had been so challenging for us to work with back then. I learned a couple had retired, but that a number of them were still on that ward, doing the same job. Can you imagine, after twelve years?

I have too many similar stories of colleagues to tell: some who got promoted purely on the basis of their skin colour, through nepotism, some who went on to fail because they lacked the judgement that could only be developed by genuine experience. They got to high positions but had a poor reputation, becoming the butt of jokes and subject of gossip.

Here are a few key lessons I learned from these and other people-related experiences, which have enabled my resilience over the years.

1. Don't take things personally

At times, people behave in ways you don't understand. There could be any number of explanations for their behaviour – none of which actually have anything to do with you.

This is a colourful old life, and it's filled with a rather interesting ensemble of characters. There are grumpy people, angry people, racist people, broken people, greedy people, uncaring people, selfish people, people who speak one value system but don't live it. At the same time, there are good people, kind people, thoughtful people, loving people, people of integrity who live the values they speak. None of these characteristics describes any one person absolutely. They manifest in varying ways and levels in individuals depending on a range of factors.

If they behave poorly towards you, it can impact on you emotionally if you take their words or attitudes personally. For example, if someone is racist, it's not because something is wrong with you, it's because something is the matter with them. So, don't take it personally. By that, I mean, do not ruminate on their behaviour; don't let it occupy your thoughts, or internalise what they say. In the next chapter I explore taking control of your thoughts and how critical this is to your mental and emotional, even your physical, health and well-being.

Allowing negative experiences to occupy your thoughts can weaken you, make you anxious or thrust you into a low mood; thereby breaking down your resilience. If you're going to think about it at all, reflect only on your own response, decide how you will respond the next time it happens – if at all. We can choose our response in the face of conflict or adversity. No one can take that power away from you, unless you give them that power.

I've been stopped by the police on two occasions while driving. Neither time had I done anything that warranted the aggression that was spewed at me. Both times, I chose my response carefully. I obeyed their every instruction. I spoke gently, quietly when asked a question. I didn't ask why they stopped me,

nor did I argue with them. As the exchange went on and I continued in that demeanour, I heard their tones begin to change drastically. They became conversational – respectful. The second time, I did feel irritated, as being stopped and ordered to stand at the side of the road was making me late for work. But by the time I had finished with those three police officers, I had managed to share my faith in Jesus Christ with one of them, heard how her son was becoming a challenging teenager at home; and that maybe she should try taking him to church – even if she wasn't 'quite ready to get as serious about Jesus' as I sounded. When at last they gave me permission to go, I leaned over and hugged the female police officer and she hugged me back! Can you believe that? As I've said before, racism is an ignorance and a madness!

2. Human opinion is fickle

Human opinion can put you on a pedestal, and topple you from the same pedestal, in the same day. Opinions and attitudes change with the regularity of the tides of the sea. If you build your identity or how you feel about yourself based on other people's opinions, your moods will be as unstable.

Again, I draw from the example of Christ's own experience of public opinion. One day the people lined the streets and shouted 'Hosanna!', hailing him as their king (pedestal) as he rode past minding his own business. He hadn't organised the celebration, but the people had heard of his great exploits in other towns and got excited. Five days later, the same crowds shouted, 'Crucify him!' (toppled from pedestal), through no fault of his own. Seriously, you do yourself injury if you allow your emotional and mental well-being to be strongly influenced by what others say or do – particularly in competitive environments such as the workplace.

3. Always have a plan

We take control of our state, our lives and our future when we stop waiting for others to signal to us what should happen. In the early days of my career on that ward, although I so enjoyed caring for my patients, I was, at times, a little bemused. As a young woman it was confusing, dealing with the unpredictable changes in individual attitudes. But when I heard some of the sentiments expressed by my colleagues when I was leaving, I realised I had put way too much stock in their personalities. It was a lesson I needed to learn early in my career, and I'm glad that I did. After that I decided to focus on my potential and my future. Whatever work environment I was in, I would be very clear in my mind why I was there, what I wanted to achieve (in terms of learning new skills, carrying greater responsibility and the like), and, critically, when I was going to leave.

This gave me great resilience when the environments were toxic. Others came to me to share their stories and I would listen, then say, 'You need to have a plan.' So much so, that it became a kind of slogan. They'd come back and say, 'She said this, but it's fine, because I have a plan!' Or, 'I'm working on my plan!' We laughed, but in fact that redirection of attention, that taking ownership over one's responses and future, is very empowering, and a principal strategy for building resilience and boosting mood.

On the train back to London after meeting those former colleagues at that conference, I took the opportunity to reflect. I saw that those scary people who had once featured so largely in one phase of my life, had become so small that they no longer featured at all. My life and career had moved on, but they were still where I left them those many years ago. In a way, their lot seemed a little tragic. Yet it's the lot they chose.

Bullying, harassment, belittling and undermining others are all features of the same mindset as insecurity, low self-esteem, envy and a sense of entitlement, which can leave those with that mindset stagnant and miserable. The only way they can feel better about themselves is by pulling down other people. I can't imagine that anyone who treats others with routine unkindness is a truly happy person.

Similarly, looking to others, blaming others, wanting others to do something, change something, and thinking then you will be happy is also a recipe for a miserable life. This comes about when we won't take ownership of our feelings and futures.

Winning or losing in life comes down to what you choose to value. You can be on top of the world, have titles, money, status, but if you're miserable, what does all that actually matter? If you are of poor reputation, then your title is an empty one and in fact will attract ridicule. Status, title, wealth and decency are not mutually exclusive. Titles, status and wealth are bonuses; Inner peace, joy, a clear conscience, releasing my potential, walking in purpose, knowing I am doing good and causing no harm to others are what amount to a meaningful and worthwhile existence. These are what make for desirable quality of life.

Be aware of the real issues of life. What do you value most? What are your goals in the long term? Make your decisions based on what matters most to you, but choose what matters most carefully. Walk a straight path. Have a plan. Do what you do, to the best of your ability. Walk in integrity. Keep your head down. Let the chips fall where they may. No one can claim ownership of you then. This is liberty. You'll bounce back every time when trouble strikes, as it inevitably will from time to time.

4. ACCEPT THAT LIFE JUST ISN'T PERFECT AND NEVER WILL BE

I don't know. Maybe it was because I was told all those stupid fairy tales (none of which was about little black girls, by the way – why I ever imagined a prince would one day ride in, sweep me off my feet, then take me to live in his palace I don't know). Maybe it's because I was a Brownie. Maybe it's because all my role models walked around looking like nothing bad ever happened them. Maybe it's the TV shows and films I watched, the books I read. But I don't know how I arrived at the idea that, at some point, everything would fall perfectly into place the way I wanted, and that I would live happily ever after.

I think back to the good old days when, as a teenager, my biggest problem in life was figuring out ways to circumvent my mother's rules. Back then it seemed like Mom had nothing better do than control my life! 'Where are you going?' 'Who with?' 'Be home by 10 p.m!' 'You can't wear that to go out!' 'It's past midnight; turn down the music!' I simply couldn't wait to turn 18 (well, 21 really. In the Caribbean 21 is the unofficial age of adulthood; and if you're unmarried and still living with your parent/s, you're treated as though you're 4!). Surely, once I was officially an adult, all, and I mean ALL, my problems would be over, and at last life would be perfect. It's been 30-plus years since I turned 18, and unless you are pubescent, you'll know from your own experience that life didn't go the way I expected!

Dad used to say, 'Don't be in such a hurry to grow up. Enjoy your childhood.' I get exactly what he meant!

At 15 I migrated; shipped off to boarding school. I still recall my very first day stomping through two-feet-deep snow in the Canadian winter between the girls' dorm and Leland Hall for my first class. The sun hadn't even thought about coming up yet, let alone shining. At 21 I migrated again – this time to England. I had to navigate new cultures. I discovered my skin colour (even my gender) could be an issue for idiots.

I had to go to university. I had to apply for visas. I had to prove this, prove that, to immigration authorities. I had to work crappy jobs. I had to find affordable places to live. I had to adjust to moving into accommodation with strangers and sharing a toilet with them! I had to provide my own food. I had to learn to live under grey skies. Problems! Problems! Problems! (But all good, because I understood they were getting me to where I wanted to go.)

In no time at all I discovered that life, although good fun, was not perfect. Adulting brought a shedload of problems – of the type even dear old mom hadn't imagined (having never migrated). Life didn't even humour my naiveté by waiting until I turned 18. Pre-empting three years, it charged at me with both horns from age 15.

So, here's the thing: personal resilience can grow from the point you accept that life isn't perfect and will never, ever be. That those inconvenient little occurrences commonly referred to as 'problems' or 'change' come in all sorts of shapes and sizes and are an unavoidable part of living – indeed, even of progress.

It'll end a life of disappointment striving for the impossible, i.e. the perfect life (whatever that is). It'll end any paranoia that you might just be the target of some cosmic hate campaign that singles you out for problems. You'll be able to exhale in the liberating knowledge that COVID was not created specifically to drive you bonkers by quarantining you for months on end with your kids. Quite a lot of your frustrations will end.

It may even stop you imagining that you are the centre of the universe and that your comfort and contentment should be the top priority (the perfect life!) for other people.

The other wonderfully exhilarating, positively mood-lifting, blues-busting, resilience-boosting effect it may have is enabling you to adjust to new, more realistic, more achievable dreams. You may even want to redefine what the 'perfect' life looks like for you, given the absolute tons of apparently unavoidable crap being slung at you on a daily basis, just as I have. You can begin this new and exciting way of thinking by abandoning any idea that we might ever fully go back to life as we knew it pre-COVID. As problematic as it is, the new normal looks like it will hang about for the foreseeable future. I would also hazard a guess that the move to a more digitally based existence will only advance, not decrease. For many, this is far from 'perfect'.

So, there are problems and then there are problems. My resilience and well-being are served when I choose to focus on only those problems I can actually resolve. As for the ones that are genuinely beyond my influence, I adjust to living with them if I have no choice, otherwise I let them go or walk away. I do not bang my head against brick walls.

When you get really skilled at this 'life's not perfect' way of thinking thing, you might even start thinking 'so what?' more often, depending on the type of problem that arises. This 'so what?' kind of thinking might look a bit like this:

So what if we're now facing something called 'The New Normal'? (I thought everybody liked 'new' things.)

So what if the government tells you to wear a face mask when you go out? (I'd much rather wear a mask than be admitted to hospital and hooked up to a ventilator.)

So what if you've got to wash your hands regularly? (Personally, I've always considered that a brilliant idea, even before COVID.)

So what if you have to do more online? (It saves a lot of time!)

So what if you have to learn some new technology? (It's not as difficult as it might first appear, and it can be fun.) I've attended more events online than I would have if I had to travel across London (or fly across the Atlantic) to get to them!

So what if you put on weight because of lockdown? (...a bit too far – 'so what?' thinking has it limits, sorry.)

Clearly, it's not applicable to every problem, but definitely can be applied to many. This strategy is meant to let you know what to do about the problems that are just not worth getting stressed over. I'm not flippant about the new normal. I'm not saying it's not problematic. It is a real pain in the rear end in many ways. What I'm saying is the new normal can be viewed as a new set of problems that you and I can both overcome, just like we've overcome problems in the past.

5. CREATE YOUR HAPPY SPACE

With the notion of a perfect life thoroughly trashed, you can build your resilience by turning your attention to creating the next best thing. My quality of life improved by leaps since the day I understood no one else is responsible for my happiness, well-being or circumstances – one of my most powerful epiphanies ever. It liberated me from much angst, frustration and stress knowing that I could take control, in large part, over my joy, peace, progress and what I achieved. For me, it was empowering to understand that fundamentally, the responsibility for those things lay squarely upon my own shoulders. I get that this might be a scary thought for some.

It is probably even the reason many prefer to look outside themselves for the source of their unhappiness. It's the government, it's immigrants, their spouse, their boss, or any number of things. But I think if we would give ourselves the permission to take responsibility for our own well-being, as far as we are able to do so, we would see a host of improvements in our experience of life. More and more, as I have, you will enjoy the life you have, love who you are, and therefore, do what you need to do to create a good present and secure the best future for you.

Empowered by this way of thinking, I set about creating my happy space – my perfectly imperfect life. My happy space is created of specific visions supported by action plans to boost my financial, mental, physical and spiritual resilience. When problems appear, my happy place is the measure against which I decide if I'm dealing with a 'so what?' kind of a problem or one that is worthy of my time and energy. My happy space isn't a place: it's a movement. It involves working on problems that truly matter to me and looks something like this (not in order of importance):

1. Financial stability, and ultimately, independence
2. Life-nourishing friendships and relationships
3. A healthier body

4. Inspiring and giving others the tools to create their own happy space through my writing, teaching and coaching (my 'life's work' or 'legacy')
5. Growing spiritually (by this I mean in character; maturing in my relationship with God)
6. Rest and recreation (I do so love this one!)

Working on these five areas every day produces immense resilience; even tiny steps in advancing them bring barrels of joy. So what's your happy space? Is it time to redesign it? After all, your happy space is supposed to make you exactly what it says on the tin – happy.

There was so much going on in my life that seemed to contribute to me feeling low. From my late twenties and throughout my thirties, I was in constant pain due to a condition called endometriosis. I was put on hormone treatments, that didn't work. I then had two oper ations, banking all my hope on the surgeon, a specialist, to bring an end to my chronic pain. Both surgeries worked for a while, but the pain returned in under a year each time. I felt depressed, hopeless about it. Why couldn't the doctor cure me? Why hadn't science found a way to deal with this? What did I do to deserve living in chronic pain? I was obsessed with finding a cure, when

there wasn't any. It was like hitting my head against a brick wall.

This was almost two decades ago. Today, I can't remember when last I had endometriosis pain. That's because one day I just stopped. I stopped obsessing about it. I stopped talking about it. I stopped going to the doctor about it. I stopped complaining about it. I stopped looking to others to help me. I even stopped taking painkillers every day, because they started burning a hole in the lining of my stomach. Looking back, I can't tell you a particular date when I stopped having endometriosis pain. All I know is that it's been years and I don't recall when last I had it.

Thoughts and words are creative material

I stopped letting it dominate me and, in so doing, it shrunk, losing its significance in my life. When I turned my attention and mind to other more fruitful things, the problem was no longer problematic. Whatever you give your attention to, grows. This was different to denial. I remember thinking and saying out loud, 'Endometriosis, stop bothering me. I'm getting on with my life.' It became a daily mantra whenever that pain reared its ugly head. I literally spoke back to it.

I believe in the Bible, and what the scripture does say is that our worlds are created and shaped by our words (paraphrase). It's like saying, if your life was a house, your thoughts and words would be the bricks and mortar with which it's built. So, if things aren't going the way you want and it's making you feel down, check your words. You might well be speaking the problem into existence and keeping it alive, just because of your confession. We live in the words we think and speak; let's choose them carefully. Practise speaking life, health, wealth, wholeness and success. Create the quality of life you prefer to have.

This strategy, is meant to encourage you to be careful about what you 'speak'; to speak life, healing, strength and wellness into your life, when you may not be feeling well or undergoing treatment for illness. As a former specialist nurse in gynaecological cancer genetics, I do want to state that even though I've shared my personal story above, I am not saying people should ignore any symptoms they may have. If you are experiencing persistent symptoms of any kind, mental or physical, my advice is that you seek appropriate advice – speak with your doctor about them.

7. EMBRACE CHANGE

There's still quite a lot of avoidance with some people regarding digital technologies. Change might feel scary because it nudges us out of comfort zones, or we don't know what the future might look like or what its impact will be on us. However, resisting inevitable change can deplete you emotionally and reduce your resilience.

I remember when mobile (or cell) phones first appeared on the market, I had no interest or appetite for them at all. When they transitioned into 'smartphones', I mocked them. I wore the fact that I didn't own one like a badge of honour! I saw it as an invasion of privacy. I finally got one because of pressure from friends. I didn't want to be left out of the loop (it's amazing what peer pressure can do!). It didn't take long for me and the phone to become inseparable.

My attitude was the same with social media. Little did I know that it would give me access to the world in a way I had never dreamt. Because I embraced the technology, I have had contact with people in Australia, New Zealand, India, Africa, South America, and places I have not even visited. I even reconnected with old an old boyfriend who migrated down under (he's the one I probably should not have let get away).

But now? Perish the thought that I should ever have to live without digital communications technology!

Digital technology is already featuring hugely since the pandemic first struck the world. This trend is set to continue. I suspect there'll be no turning back. The people who know about money are saying, invest in Tech: robotics, fintech, e-learning – it's all about tech. Online retailers and services boomed during the lockdown. Millions of people worked effectively from home using laptops and smartphones, communicating online. Kids went to school online. For us, the people, this wasn't perfect, and for many it was hugely problematic, yet still it's the shape of the future. It translates into enormous overhead savings for both commercial and public sector organisations. So, the problem isn't going to go away. It calls on us to create our happy space within the new context. Increasing your knowledge and understanding of the new normal will build your resilience and ability to adapt and cope with the inevitable changes it will bring to our daily lives.

Back when I was feeling low, I had begun to look at my life, concluding that I was not making any real progress towards finding and fulfilling my purpose in life. Purpose is a foundation stone to our health and well-being as a whole – especially our emotional and mental well-being. I reached the conclusion that I had to make some important changes. However, I was too scared to make those changes. I had been in my comfort zone so long that I didn't even know where to begin! So, I put off taking any steps towards change for a number of reasons.

For example, it was scary; what would people think; I didn't know what direction to take; I might fail. Was I even good enough, confident enough? What if this? What if that? The list went on and on. And guess what? I stayed put. But the issues never went away. I felt stifled. I knew I was capable of more. I had passion for something entirely different. Yet, I rejected making the change that was required. I saw many others living their dream life. I called them eagles. They were championing causes, moving up the career ladder, making a difference to other people's lives. I was inspired. But I let fear keep me on lockdown. This weighed heavily on me. It was depressing.

Refusing to make necessary changes to your life when you are dissatisfied or unhappy with the current state of your life will inevitably take a toll on your emotional and mental well-being. If you know you need to make a change, do it. Make a commitment to yourself to embrace that change, doing whatever is required. Just like there is a lot of information out there to increase your knowledge, there is also a lot of support available to help you. Coaching, mentoring, courses, just or having conversations with the right people, all help. There is only one life. It is precious. It is wonderful. Don't waste another hour without finding meaning in it. Don't waste another day not enjoying it.

I eventually set about making the changes I needed to in those areas of my life that were not bearing the right fruit. I accessed coaching and mentorship, which made all the difference. Life has blossomed ever since. My only regret is that I didn't make the changes sooner!

There's nothing quite like living a purposeful life, making a difference and championing the causes close to one's heart. To let passion get you up out of bed every morning. To look forward to resuming your life's work each new day. To savour every moment you spend walking in purpose. To have to force yourself to stop your work each night. That is the kind of life that's worth living, as far as I am concerned! That's my happy space. And it is achievable for each of us if we are willing to make the changes necessary.

An amazing life awaits you outside your comfort zone.

8. DEVELOP YOUR SELF-KNOWLEDGE AND AWARENESS

Mindfulness is an increasingly popular set of techniques which are really quite effective in helping people to take control and have a better experience of life. It's rooted in self-awareness.

Discovering the underlying cause of my ongoing anxiety and low mood was a game changer for me. It was the starting point for change, which ultimately set me on the road to wellness. I definitely delayed this by trying to sweep the issue under the carpet but, without knowing what it was, I would have never been able to eventually bounce back as well as I have done; or maintain my well-being.

I saw a doctor privately about my low mood. I was ashamed to see my GP. I've since learned that many people feel this way. The stigma of mental health challenges often prevents people obtaining the help they need. The doctor was called Helen and I found her on Google, using search words like, 'Christian therapist', 'Christian Counsellor' and 'Christian Psychiatrist'. That they needed to be Christian was important, because the impression I got from 'church' was that emotional or mental health challenges were spiritual. I'd heard phrases like, 'A depressed Christian is an unbalanced Christian.' Or, 'You can't be a true a Christian if you're depressed.' Plus, I was a little suspicious of psychiatry. To my thinking, my best bet was to find someone who represented both.

Helen was kind. She lived in a huge house on a leafy street in an upscale part of west London. She saw her clients in an intimate little consulting room at the front of the house, just beyond the front door. When she saw me, Helen sat in one corner furthest from the door, with her back to the wall. I sat in a chair that was positioned next to the door, across from her with my back to the door. My understanding of mental health was so poor back then. Once or twice I mused that she should sit near the door in consultation with patients, in case things got out of hand. Instead, she would be trapped in a corner with a client between her and the door! Where we get these ideas about mental health issues is really the subject for an entire book on its own. The stigma they create hinders many people from accessing the help they need.

Anyway, I liked Helen. She spoke in really soothing tones and seemed to be truly listening. On the other hand, she kept referring to, 'When you lived in Jamaica...' when asking me questions about my childhood, even though I had told her several times I was born and raised in Trinidad. One night, I corrected her for what seemed the umpteenth time: 'Trinidad. I spent my childhood in Trinidad.' She paused and said, 'Oh yes, of course, Trinidad! How do you find it when I keep saying Jamaica?' To which I replied, 'I find it tedious.' She chuckled and I could see she was genuinely amused. 'Yes, I'm sure it must be tedious,' she answered.

I always recall that as being a funny moment for us – perhaps the only funny moment, as I literally spent each hour with her, twice sometimes three times per month, for six months, crying. I have to admit that I'm giggling now as I recall that exchange. Hey, it worked. After that, Jamaica never featured in my therapy again! (Although some of my Jamaican friends would probably say it should have!) Some people would argue that it's not racist to assume every Caribbean person must be Jamaican, but actually, it is – especially when you keep telling someone you aren't but they insist that you must be (after all, you're black!).

I once escorted an elderly patient from one hospital to another. She was pleasant to spend the half a day with. She asked me where I was from. I replied, 'I was born in Trinidad.' 'Trinidad?' she looked at me quizzically. 'Yes, it's in the Caribbean; you know, the West Indies.' I said, thinking I was helping. Her face lit up, as some sort of penny finally dropped. 'Oh, you mean Jamaica!' I had to give her a quick geography lesson to get her up to speed.

I don't know how helpful or not those six months with Helen turned out to be for me in terms of my getting better – but that's mainly because I wasn't actually ready to take on board her diagnosis of what was wrong. Plus, it was exhausting. All I did was cry. I literally went through a box of tissues every time. So much so, I asked if I should start bringing my own boxes. Helen simply smiled and said that it wasn't necessary, in her kindly voice.

There was one session that really did help me articulate all the strange feelings I had been experiencing in the months before coming to see her, though. And that is the critical point at which all the other sessions enabled me to arrive.

In some of our sessions, she took me to shelves filled with toys and asked me to select any that I wanted. Other times she asked me to choose from lumps of play dough. I would then be instructed to shape it into something that represented how I felt.

Some years later, I was a co-collaborator on a research project that assessed the impact of handling museum artefacts on patients enabling them to speak about how they felt about their cancer. Our theory was that the handling of objects diffused anxiety, freeing people to then access their memories and speak openly about their experiences when they otherwise found it difficult to do so spontaneously.

Anyway, the technique did work on me while I was Helen's patient because it helped put what I was going through into words for the very first time, when all I could do previously, was cry.

On one such evening, I chose a black lump and moulded it into a bowl-like structure that was very wide at the surface, narrowing a bit at the base. It was a very deep bowl. I then made a little person and positioned it on the inside wall of the bowl, somewhere about a third of the way down. Helen said, 'Now describe it; talk me through this.'

I told her that I felt like I was in a big black hole. There was a time in my life when the hole itself hadn't existed for me, or at least, I didn't know it was there.

Then at some point, I found myself sitting on the edge of it looking in, not knowing what it was or what it represented. It looked like an abyss of darkness so blinding, that I could see nothing else. For a long time I didn't know what to do about it, so I just kept holding on to the surface edge as best I could.

The inner surface of the hole was very slippery (and still is, but I've learned how to create traction). I was sliding downwards.

At the point of seeing her, I wasn't very far down, but I was getting exhausted.

'Exhausted by what?' Helen asked me.

'Tired of holding myself up. I'm slipping down further every day and I'm tired of holding on.'

'What would happen if you let go?'

'If I let go, I'd fall right to the bottom. I don't think I'd be able to climb back out.'

Thank God, to this day, I have never slipped to the bottom of that hole. With the right help, I learned how to defy gravity. I am armed with an arsenal of tools that enable me to respond effectively when that gaping hole beckons. I have learned to gather my strength again and choose to step back into the light when the condition causes me to drift out of it.

More than a decade later, I haven't forgotten the hole. It is still the measure I use to assess where I am in relation to depression. It appears vaguely like a crouching predator that stalks way over in the distance. Like something you glimpse out of the corner of your eye. It's not near, but I know it's there. And it knows I'm here.

My job is to preserve the distance that exists between us as best I can. All the strategies I'm sharing here are what I use to keep it at bay.

Self-knowledge is the starting point for more effective self-care and increased self-mastery.

Yours doesn't have to be a story of depression to benefit from developing a better knowledge of yourself. When you are feeling low in mood, spend some time observing the types of thoughts that come to your mind, your way of processing them, how they affect you and how you respond to what you're thinking and what is happening around you. Get to know yourself really well. Become aware of your personal triggers, which then result in dips in your mood. Be sensitive to your feelings and know when a dip is coming. Learn how to manage it.

From personal experience, I've learned that feeling low can be managed effectively; you don't have to let it overtake you. Good management begins with self-awareness: taking a moment to check your 'state' and reflecting on what's going on in your thoughts, your environment, or circumstance, to identify what's triggering it. Usually, it's simply because I'm physically and mentally drained. Then I look back and realise I've gone for weeks working seven days, juggling all the different strands I'm involved in. In this post-millennial world, it's easy to get very busy and caught up with life. My remedy is to time out at the nearest opportunity. I rest, sleep, watch movies. I simply escape to quiet my mind and recharge my body anywhere from an entire weekend to a week. Sooner or later, I can feel myself coming back to the surface and feel the light shining on my face again.

There is just so much to learn about yourself. The more you know and understand about who you are, what drives you, what you value, what you despise, the better.

I have always been a quiet, introspective person. I enjoy spending long hours on my own. During those times I read, sketch, write, play music. I've been this way since my early childhood. Often, I was judged or criticised for it, called 'moody', 'dreamer', 'reserved', 'unfriendly'; I was even accused of being a snob by a close relative. On some level I started to believe something was wrong with me. I felt rejected and began to reject myself.

Mine is a family of extroverts. I was in my late twenties when I discovered that my seeming 'aloofness' wasn't that something was wrong with me. It was simply other people's interpretation of my temperament. I was an introvert. These characteristics – being on the quiet side, thinking a lot, introspection, needing time on one's own – were typical of that temperament.

A simple distinction between people who have an introverted versus an extroverted temperament is that the latter are energised by having lots of company, whereas the former are energised being alone. Extroverts need some time out, but not for extended periods. If you're one, avoid isolating yourself completely. If you're an introvert, never retreating to replenish your energy will erode your resilience.

During the lockdown period, I often wondered about people's living situations and how well (or not) introverts, with no private space to retreat to and recharge, coped if they were living with extroverts. Likewise, I was concerned for extroverted friends who lived alone; and made an effort to make regular contact with them.

These two temperaments can give rise to conflict in relationships if they are not understood. The world needs them both. In fact, a large proportion of the great leaders in history were known introverts.

This is a simple skimming of the surface of these temperaments. There is so much more to learn about them. There are loads of books written about it if you want to find out more. The subject fascinates me, because so many of my own idiosyncrasies and those of my friends, loved ones and colleagues, become clear when you recognise their temperament. It's enabled me to meet my own emotional, mental and social needs, and those of others, with greater effectiveness.

Understanding the richness of your particular temperament – whether it is introversion or extroversion and how it affects your life, relationships and overall well-being – is worth paying some attention to.

9. CREATE A MEMORY BANK OF GOOD MEMORIES

A collection of good memories, which release joy and pleasure, even pride, can be very useful in those moments when you're feeling down. For example, it could be a memory of something you achieved, a wise decision you made, time spent with loved ones, a good meal out with friends, a time when you did well in a situation.

Reflecting on good or positive memories will change your outlook and boost your resilience. They can get you up and running again with renewed joy and energy.

At the height (or depth) of my depression, my mind went round and round the same old

thoughts – bad memories. Those memories comprised mistakes, failures, embarrassments, painful things that were said to me, things I had lost, etc. Such thoughts drained my energy, robbing me of my joy and chipping away at my resilience. I slipped further and further down into the black hole of despair.

Reliving good memories has the opposite effect. Good memories create enjoyment. They empower, encourage and build confidence.

Music and memory can be a heady combination in some cases. In the next section I suggest that music is a powerful therapy, mentioning my 'top ten best songs of all time' list. Number one on that list is a song I liked as a teenager, but fell in love with one night when I was about 18. I was at a wine bar with my friend Hayden. I remember that song came on their system and filled the dark, dreamy space. Hayden asked me to dance. I still remember him leading me round the dancefloor. We were completely chilled. I felt relaxed and happy in that moment. It's a memory I still cherish and is always guaranteed to put a smile on my face. Another music memory that transports me back to happy times is driving with my grandfather. He had those massive eight-track tapes that he played. I still remember a song now called *Both Sides*, which forever framed those wonderful occasions in my memory.

10. PLAY YOUR FAVOURITE MUSIC

I am not sure exactly when music dropped out of my life. But I love music, and when I added it back to my life, it brought a breath of fine, fresh air.

I love music across a wide range of genres. I have particular pieces of music that I absolutely adore. It's inevitable that when I play some of my favourite music, my spirits will lift. Resilience is boosted through enjoyment. Sometimes we need to intentionally do what we enjoy.

I've got a 'top ten songs of all time' list. If you don't have such a list, why not compile one, just for the fun of it? Just spending some time pondering over

that is bound to perk you up. You may even feel excited, and that's a wonderful feeling to have. Hey, you may even dance! I don't think it's possible to still feel low in mood after losing oneself dancing to your favourite music.

Music got me through some tough times in life. Writing my dissertation one summer, I played a single song over and over again. It literally kept me company, pulling me back from breaking point as I worked sometimes up to 14 or 15 hours per day trying to get it done in time for submission.

Music can both soothe or excite the soul.

11. WATCH A GOOD FILM

Like my top ten music list, I have a top ten movies and TV shows of all-time list. I don't necessarily watch these all the time. But at times, a scene or a quote might pop to mind and that affects me positively.

Bouncing back is largely about focusing on what you enjoy and allowing yourself to savour and relive experiences that brought you a sense of joy and well-being.

What's in your top ten list of films and TV?

From personal experience, I'm all too aware of the overwhelming toll worry,

anxiety or sadness exert on your emotional, psychological and physical well-being.

A bit of escapism can go a long way to resetting your mood. Coming back to the reality of life, you may feel stronger, more energised and better able to tackle the issues facing you.

12. BE INTENTIONAL ABOUT LAUGHTER

So many good things can happen when we are intentional about them. That includes laughter.

During my denial phase, I was aware that people were noticing my generally downcast air. To not worry my parents, family and friends, I pasted on a smile to mask my despair.

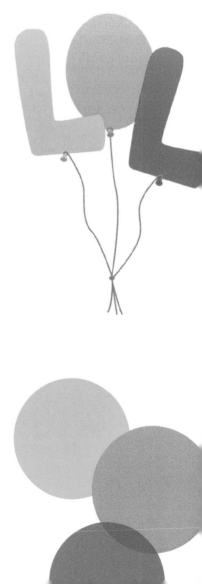

It's difficult trying to make people comfortable around you when you're struggling on the inside to keep from falling apart; to put on a smile, when the very life is being sucked out of you and you're slipping down into a black hole. But there is still hope. I know there is hope. I see so many reasons to hope around me. Although at times I felt hopeless, there is a part of me that has never lost hope.

I have acquired a learned optimism over the years, and that has enabled my resilience. Even in trying times, life provides us with ample opportunities for laughter. As serious and demanding as life is, it is at the same time quirky, dead weird and hilarious. Life doesn't let any of us escape its drama. Don't let the weirdness or hilarity be dead to you. Spot it and laugh at it. It will diffuse your tension. In some cases, it may even change what looked insurmountable to you, suddenly manageable.

Laughter makes good medicine.

13. REMEMBER, YOUR MOODS ARE FLEETING

Moods are not permanent. They pass. You may feel down one day, but the next day bounce back to feeling more positive. The best thing is to not make any major decisions during a time when you're down.

A mood is a feeling that you can change

Emotions shift throughout the course of the day. Thinking 'this too will pass' is a way of not letting your emotions control your life. A great way to manage or change your mood to a lighter, more positive one is laughter. Watching a good comedy can be like taking a pill. Reading something that gives you a good laugh can work like an elixir. Remembering something funny can be like a healing balm. Whatever the source, be intentional about laughter, like you would be about taking a pill. Savour a deep belly laugh. Laugh 'til the water falls from your eyes. Laugh until the muscles of your cheeks ache. You will feel better afterwards.

14. SPEND TIME WITH PEOPLE YOU LOVE OR WHO YOU ENJOY BEING WITH

In a later section, I share how choosing two good friends to talk to about depression helped me. I've kept it separate from this section because they are indeed distinct. The people you choose to go to when you're feeling low are a subset of those you enjoy spending time with. Not everyone you enjoy spending time with has the capacity to be the person you can safely bare your soul to.

So, when I say spend time with people you love and also enjoy being with or people who make you feel good, what I mean is exactly that. Be wary of those whose words, attitudes and actions don't

inspire your confidence, joy, positivity, peace or desire to achieve your goals or dreams. Be cautious of those in whose company you can't be yourself. Those types will always be around. In protecting your emotional and mental well-being, you are not powerless. You have the power to decide for yourself the extent to which you allow them to influence you and shape your outlook.

I want to include a caveat regarding family. We can choose who we have as friends, but not who our family are. We love our relatives, but it's not always easy to like them. The fact that you are of the same family does not oblige you to tolerate or accept abusive behaviours, habitual disrespect or oppression from another person.

Families are a dynamic and complex set relationships. These can be as fulfilling and life giving, as destructive and harmful to mental well-being. Highly complicated relationships are well beyond the scope of this book. All I will say here is that nothing changes without constructive, informed and wise action.

One powerful action any of us can take is that of being more intentional about self-care to build and maintain emotional and mental well-being.

Harsh words or abusive treatment are not reflections of your innate value.

It's important to your emotional and mental health and well-being to understand that when someone is abusive towards you, it is not your responsibility. They are fully responsible for their behaviour. They are responsible for whatever they choose to say, whatever they choose to do, and whatever they choose not to do that they rightly should do. What they say or how they treat you is not a reflection of your innate value or worth.

My personal view is that we should avoid toxic relationships. That includes relatives. Do whatever you can to resolve issues: let them know you love them, that you want to have a good relationship with them. Also let them know how their words, behaviours and attitudes affect you. Give it some time. However, if things don't improve, give them some space. Reduce your exposure to anyone who has nothing good to say to you or about you. Decrease contact with anyone who habitually undermines your self-confidence or self-belief or negatively impacts your sense of worth. Do not take to heart what is said.

There are instances when our own words or behaviours have offended others and hurt our relationships. This can manifest in open resentment, or even abuse. If you have tried to reconcile and seek forgiveness but they refuse to forgive, bless them and move on. Keep the door open to them coming back into your life when they feel ready, but until then, give them time. Nothing is gained by further aggravating the situation.

I think kids are funny and cute, so I'm only too happy to spend time with my friends' kids or kids in my family. I like people who have a sense of humour, so I spend time with them because I laugh a lot.

I love being with people of a compassionate nature, who are fair, whose humility hangs about them like a beautiful fragrance. They inspire me to be my best.

They say people with depression are depressed because they pick up on the emotions of others – their secret pains and sorrows; they sense much of what is wrong in the world. I'm inclined to agree. I don't have to know you to empathise on a deep level with your plight. My heart is bruised for people I don't know and will never meet, who live in difficult places and circumstances. Some of the sadness I experience is linked to their vulnerability, their potential being limited, the likelihood that their hopes, dreams and aspirations may never be realised. I'm saying this to say that being in the company of people who care about what I care about is like coming out from under the burning sun to stand in the shade. Seek the company of people who share your values and have respect for others regardless of rank. Spending time with people whose values are different gives rise to conflict and unnecessary hurt and upset. Choose the people with whom you spend time with greater care.

A final point that I wish to make before I move on to the next chapter, is that being alone also comes with many terrific benefits. I spend large amounts of time alone, which is a natural function of my introverted temperament. While I enjoy the company of my friends and family, I thoroughly enjoy my own company. Time alone is a priority for me. I appreciate that if you're an extrovert, you may feel differently. Solitude is different from loneliness; people can feel lonely even in the company of others. So, there is something about learning how to enjoy one's self. Arriving at your own authentic balance of contentment. Savouring the experience of life and living, from your centre, outward, rather than outward, in. Tapping into the richness of who you are as an individual human being. Drawing on your inner treasury of resources, so you are content whether you are by yourself, or in a crowd. Becoming your own best friend; comfortable in solitude. Later on, I write something on faith. To me, nurturing this sense of internal wellbeing and contentment, independent of circumstance, is one of the key pillars of having a faith. Whether your world couldn't be better, or if it's falling apart, your strength is rooted in this. Learning to be comfortable in solitude may help decrease any feelings of loneliness, particularly in times of isolation during lockdown.

15. PRACTICE GRATITUDE

When you're feeling low, it's easy to forget what's working well for you. The mind focuses on those things that are not working well. During the lockdown, you may have experienced a number of things not working well. You may have lost your job or had a bereavement of a friend or relative, for example.

Count your blessings

In troubling times, it helps to take time out; to step back from the melee, the drama of life falling apart, for a few minutes every day. In those minutes, shift your thoughts inwardly. Think about what you do have, what is good, what is working well. It could be as basic as, 'I woke up today', 'I have my health', 'My children are safe'. Remember, too, that as bad as things might be, they could be worse. Be thankful that they aren't. You'll be amazed how redirecting your thoughts away from the negative towards the positive will change how you're feeling.

That's important, because as you begin to feel better, you move from a defeated attitude to one where you feel more hopeful. As you feel more hopeful, you become more creative. As you become more creative, your mind is better able to identify solutions to the problem that led you to feel low. In this process, your body chemistry changes and your mood is lifted. You can even feel joy again.

Like many of the strategies I share in this book, this one might take some practice before you begin to enjoy its benefits. Sadly, many of us are in the habit of viewing the world, or our lives, through negative lenses. It does take some intentional work to change the way we think, but it's more than worth the effort. Once we master this technique, it becomes 'second nature'. I do it now without even being aware; it's now a reflex for me and works every single time!

Change your thoughts

16. FOCUS ON YOUR DREAMS AND GOALS

Doing this has been the foundational piece in my recovery and maintaining my emotional and mental well-being. I wrote my first book during a tough phase, while still in denial about depression. In retrospect, I wonder what direction life would have taken had I not set this challenging goal to focus on and keep me going.

It was difficult, but I pushed through to a first draft over a six-month period. Writing is cathartic and it's an activity that comes naturally to me. I thoroughly enjoy the writing process. In the haze of a mind that felt woolly with the effects of depression, keeping this goal in focus made it possible

for me to break through to shards of light, like walking between storm clouds.

It became my one source of joy and meaning in that period. Pursuing that goal became the reason to get up every day, and keep going to work at my job. It was the reason I couldn't give up.

Others I know testify to similar experiences. There was a young woman who lost her husband and toddler daughter in a car crash. In that single moment, her entire world burnt down around her. Her boss gave her great flexibility, in terms of not coming into the office for an extended period.

However, she insisted that the young woman took on a major writing project, giving her a deadline for completion. I heard that young woman describe the experience as being extremely difficult, but having a project to work on had in fact pulled her through the darkest hour of her life. In the midst of processing her  bereavement, having a substantial goal was her only shining light at the end of the long dark tunnel of grief.

17. TREAT YOURSELF KINDLY

Without intending to, we may be treating ourselves with much less kindness and consideration than we would treat others. In the business of life, people habitually neglect themselves. We don't get enough sleep. We don't take sufficient time out to rest and refresh when we need to. We push our weariness to one side, forcing ourselves to keep going. We build up high levels of stress and ignore all the signs.

Depression forced me to take stock of all these health-damaging behaviours I engaged in and become intentional in self-care. Much of what I'm sharing in this book are my techniques for self-care. They serve me well. I no longer take my health and well-being for granted; I take my self-care very seriously.

Our bodies are very good at letting us know when we are abusing them. Our emotions are also excellent indicators that we have crossed the line. For instance, irritability can be a symptom of tiredness. Feeling low or 'under the weather' can also be symptomatic of fatigue that is not addressed. In fact, it can also be a sign of serious physical illness.

Self-care is very important in preventing anxiety or low moods. It is certainly essential to building resilience or boosting your mood.

Therefore, one kindness we should be affording ourselves is acknowledging the way we feel – physically, emotionally, mentally. Take note of what is happening to your emotions and in your body. It didn't help me at all being in denial when I was feeling unwell.

Feeling low may result from pushing yourself too hard, overworking, worrying, stress and many other reasons. Give yourself the space to work out the root of why you may be feeling anxious or why your mood is low. From there you can decide on the appropriate course of action to turn things around. It is reasonable to say 'No' to things that add stress and unhappiness to your life. Women are notoriously reticent about putting helpful, health-protecting boundaries in place. As we get older, our bodies and minds will demand it from us!

As you might imagine, I had the chance to meet several hundred, if not thousands, of people while working as a nurse in a number of hospitals and other healthcare settings. Some come and go within hours; others can remain on the wards for weeks. There are lots of opportunities to get into conversation with them, get to know them as people. Many of them openly share their deepest fears, their greatest joys as well as their regrets, pains and sorrows with you their 'nurse'.

I got into one such conversation with a beautiful young woman one evening on the ward. She looked really downcast, so I asked her what was wrong. The woman opened up and told me that she was dreading being discharged and returning home. This surprised me, because I had met her husband and some of her relatives when they came to visit.

'Oh? Why is that? Your hubby seems nice,' I replied.

'Yes, he is,' she answered. 'It's not him; it's his mother. She lives with us...'.

'What about his mother?'

'Since she moved in it's been horrible. She is controlling, she undermines me, she's always complaining to him about me and now we argue a lot.'

Long story short, my patient's husband was finding it difficult to defend her against his mother. He felt a responsibility for housing his mother. Culturally, he felt his hands were tied when it came to challenging his mother or setting boundaries for her, despite the fact she was living in his and his wife's home.

I was sympathetic to her plight and suggested she needed to have a conversation with her husband, and tell him how she felt, with the expectation he would take action to resolve the situation. She was discharged the following morning. I don't know what became of her.

I shared this story to highlight how disempowered some people allow themselves to feel in their own homes, which then results in anxiety, a low mood or depression. Having the courage and confidence to speak up when you are being bullied or oppressed in any relationship is important to maintaining your emotional and mental well-being. Don't suffer in silence. Seek the help you need, preserve your safety and well-being. I share a number of tips for building self-confidence and dealing with personal fears in my book, *Do Great Exploits*.

Negative thoughts fuel anxious feelings, low mood and depression. Harbouring negative thoughts about yourself or others can steal your joy and depress your mood. Likewise, comparing yourself with others may lead to feelings of failure and inadequacy. To be kind to yourself, focus on where you want to be and recognise and celebrate just how far you've come.

Beware how you think about yourself; what you're saying to yourself in your thoughts. 'I can't...', 'I'm so stupid...', 'I'm so clumsy...', 'I'm so worthless...'. Many people would never dream of saying these types of things to another person, yet it's the way they speak to themselves all the time. Negative thoughts are like filling your swimsuit with rocks and then expecting to float when you go into the sea. They weigh you down. They bring you down.

Be kind in the way you think about yourself and others. Choose to stop the negative thoughts that bounce around your mind, and think differently. To boost and maintain a positive, feel-good mood, develop the habit of thinking good, healthy, positive things about yourself and others.

If you are holding a grudge against someone, it will inevitably cause you to feel low. Whenever that person comes to mind, you'll feel a mix of negative emotions such as anger, resentment, sadness, bitterness, perhaps even hatred. None of these will do you any good. You're feeling them doesn't hurt the other person: it hurts you. Emotions affect our body chemistry, although the link between emotions and certain diseases is still a subject being debated.

There are studies that have found a correlation between negative emotions, such as high levels of anxiety, and deaths from cancer. It is therefore wise to forgive, for your own sake, if not for the sake of the other person! Do yourself this kindness by letting go of unforgiveness, grudges, resentment and all the negative emotions they cause. Spare your body the trauma of hormone imbalances and other chemicals which are harmful to health – whether mentally or physically.

This harks back to the section on 'knowing yourself'. I want to urge you to develop your self-awareness on a very deep level. It is only then that you will come to an understanding of the things that produce certain outcomes in your life. Let the scales fall from your eyes so you can see with more clarity what might be at the root of your pain, your sadness; why you may be disappointed about your current life, riddled with fears that breed self-limiting beliefs or even lead to self-sabotage. Yes, there are external factors that we must do battle with, but largely it is our own internal, unexamined and unresolved issues of the mind that are the most powerful enemies of our progress and actualisation.

Know yourself. Then, armed with self-knowledge, free yourself from all bitter roots that bind you.

Learn to choose you. So many people sacrifice themselves, their needs, their values, their wisdom in exchange for other people so that they would not end up alone. They choose relationships that require them to actively go against what they know to be true, right, fair. Living that way erodes your self-respect, self-worth and self-confidence over time. It can result in low mood and all sorts of emotional or mental problems.

Be true to yourself

If you are not living in a way that is true to yourself, it is inevitable that you will lose joy, peace, even hope, because you have rejected yourself and your own truth. No one, no status and no amount of money is worth the emptiness such a conflict creates in the heart or soul. You want to avoid that darkened existence by choosing to walk in your truth.

Be your own coach. Coaches motivate, inspire, support, empower others. Practise doing the same for yourself.

Treat yourself to something nice, that you can afford. Retail therapy is a mood booster for many people. Be sensible about this one. If your low mood or anxiety is rooted in debt or loss of income, retail therapy might give you a boost, but it will only be short-lived, or may even worsen how you feel, because you have spent money you do not have.

My change didn't happen overnight. It was slow, like a marathon. But, hey, even though runners are slower than sprinters, they still make steady progress moving forward, don't they? That is how it was for me; facing the reality of my depression, what it could mean for me, and committing to giving myself every chance at living my life to the fullest AND enjoying every minute of it.

You've got to give yourself every chance at living your best life and believe that you are worth the effort. You must become your own best friend. Your own cheerleader. Yours shouldn't be the voice that's tearing you down. It's your voice; use it for you, not against you.

While at you're at it, help and encourage others to also live their best life. Be a voice of encouragement to those around you. Use your voice to build people up, not tear them down.

Lockdown was quite an experience. I appreciate everyone's circumstance is different and the experiences of lockdown would likely be as diverse as the people who had them.

For me, there were many benefits. It was an opportunity to do life more slowly. I had more head space. More time to reflect, think, plan, organise and reorganise, to take steps towards new projects. It gave me a taste of a life I'd never experienced before. New ways of living and being I didn't expect emerged naturally and, as a result, my quality of life improved. I cooked my own food (I had previously lived on takeaway and fast foods). I lost 20 lbs just because I cooked and ate different foods. I stayed indoors, apart from going to the grocery store once a week or walking at the local park for some fresh air. I spoke with close friends and family almost every day. I worked and was productive. The new way of living and pace of life fuelled my joy and my peace, giving me a deep sense of well-being each day. I want to hold on to many aspects of it as we come out of lockdown.

What worked well for you during lockdown? Was there anything you enjoyed? Were you able to find your peaceful place? Did it highlight your need to create a peaceful place for yourself?

I was fortunate enough to be able to work from home. At first, I felt really disorientated. In the absence of my friends and colleagues, the buzz of the office environment, the rush to get to meetings on time, the spontaneous conversations on the corridors, the quick bouncing off of ideas with colleagues, it was like being shipwrecked on a strange, uninhabited island. The contents of my email inbox made little sense to me from the isolation of my little kitchen. Suddenly, the world seemed so much larger and distant. I didn't know how to bridge the gap between me and it.

A week or so into lockdown, that black hole was beckoning.

That beast in the far corner of the field was inching nearer. I had to take control.

It was important for me to build a routine while in lockdown. So, I did. Wake up. Coffee, meditation and prayer. Get dressed: make-up, jewellery, hair done – the works. Sit at my kitchen table. Open laptop. Music playing in the background. Work. Attend meetings digitally. Eat wholesome, delicious foods. Go for a walk. Drink. Hydrate.

Routine is useful because it reduces the number of decisions we need to make. Therefore, we save emotional and mental energy for the bigger, more significant issues of life. It enables us to reserve our attention for what matters most, thereby building our resilience.

If a routine no longer works for you, break it. If it bores you or stresses you needlessly, let it go.

It's OK to do things differently if that better suits your needs. An important part of being able to bounce back is flexibility. Flexibility allows for change. It keeps you from getting stuck in a rut. It's a wonderful tool. When applied appropriately, flexibility enables you to flow harmoniously with life's changing tides.

Some folks, especially the female ones, have developed the habit of always swimming upstream. There are times when you should swim against the tide, but not every time or on every issue. Desist from always having to be right or have the final say. Learn the beautiful art of walking away, even before the argument starts.

Know when to take a stand and fight, and when to give in and flow. Choose your battles well. Choose your surrenders well too. Decide to let go in certain situations. You will have the joy of doing so.

Learn to surrender

If you routinely look after everybody, stop. Look after a few people who are closest to you. Let adults look after themselves. Let your adult children take responsibility for themselves and their decisions. To do this is love.

You are not the saviour of the world. Accept that truth. Break unhealthy helper behaviours that in the long run deplete you emotionally and create dependency, handicap maturity and hinder others from becoming responsible people. If that's the impact you're having, then you are not helping.

1.Get Some Sunlight

I live in the United Kingdom, which is famed the world over for bad weather. Most of our days in England are grey and heavy. It also rains a lot. At the slightest hint of sunshine, people get excited. Everyone comes out. Some head for the beaches, others for the many parks and natural outdoor spots, just to enjoy being in the sun. Who can blame them? I have found that being out in sunshine, especially in a natural setting, always lifts my mood.

2. Exercise

Physical activity releases many feel-good brain chemicals such as endorphins, dopamine, norepinephrine and serotonin, which boost mood and give us an exhilarating, can-do attitude. I find exercise really boring; but I do enjoy taking walks. After a brisk walk, even for 20 minutes, I feel great. Plus, I find it clears my head of clutter and removes stress, setting me up perfectly to bounce back into the pace of life. Regular exercise is definitely beneficial to regulating moods.

3. Eat Healing Foods

There are a number of foods that have been shown to improve mood in many research studies. These include green leafy vegetables, berries, oats, bananas and fermented foods, to name a few. Fortunately, I naturally love spinach and broccoli, so find it very easy to consume these with virtually every meal I have; and notice their positive effect on my energy levels and mood. I also consume loads of foods that are known to reduce inflammation in the body; drinking lemon teas and turmeric teas. Fermented milk, has also been shown in some studies to have an effect on mood by enabling better absorption of essential brain nutrients in the gut. I drink two or three table spoons of kefir milk every day.

I've noticed the difference these foods make personally, and include them in my daily diet. The Mediterranean diet is often featured as one which supports both physical and mental health. Why not do some research yourself and see what might work for you?

Near the start of lockdown, I could feel myself slipping downwards into that black hole due to all that was taking place. I immediately took action to halt that downward spiral by launching a fundraiser.

I shifted the focus off my own worries, to those of others. I set a target of £300 on one of the fundraising websites and sent the link round to family, friends, and across my social media sites.

By that afternoon, the donations had surpassed £100. That really perked me up. I was so moved by people's response. Within 24 hours, we had reached the target. I was thrilled. The next day I woke

up to find people were still giving. I let it run. In four days, we passed the £500 mark.

Keeping track of the donations and having phone calls with people about it filled me with high levels of excitement and joy, which lingered for weeks afterwards.

The money was sent overseas to support families and children affected by COVID lockdown. My partners sent back images of how the money was used. Bags of rice and food items for 80 families in The Gambia! Personal protective equipment for teachers and students at a school in the same town. I couldn't have been happier with the outcome; it blasted me right out of the black hole!

This was definitely one for my bank of good memories!

Supporting others is a really great way to decrease a sense of loneliness too. Assisting someone else with an earnest desire to lift them through some act of kindness or a compassionate word, can make them feel better. People like being around those who make them feel good. Kindness can be a bridge to a relationship. When you do something nice for someone, it can open the door to friendship.

23. FAITH

Faith helps because its basis is hope. It also provides a much wider perspective about life, meaning and one's place in a bigger picture.

I believe there is a God. There were periods when I questioned God and felt angry towards Him. I want to do so much with my life, but it is so hard sometimes due to my condition. I believe He hears me when I speak to Him; and that he responds. He may not change something that I ask Him to change, but He empowers me so that I cope better or do better. I have many memories of when I believe God did this; when mountains became mere hills, where hills became flat.

I have many testimonies of His reality through His responses to my prayers.

I did pray for healing from depression many, many, many times. I no longer ask for that. What has happened over time instead is that I have found purpose in my circumstance. I now see that my experience of depression gave me a powerful platform to help others – particularly in the area of motivation, which is where I struggled (and still do at times) the most.

I write books. I give talks. I support others. I host a talk show on radio. He's allowed it to give my life a new type, and level, of relevance. Everything I do now is about motivating and encouraging others to go forward and overcome every obstacle until they achieve whatever they want to achieve. I can speak on that with a lot of authority gained from actual experience of doing it myself. Depression forced me to become a coach. In learning to be my own motivational mindset coach, I now motivate people and coach them on mindset.

My relationship with God is central to my life. I find comfort in the reality of my experiences of His hand at work behind the scenes of my life. He is the one constant in a lifetime of change.

Why not look into this? Develop faith. Search and discover for yourself whether God is real, then get to know him.

24. TELL SOMEONE TRUSTWORTHY

I was diagnosed over 15 years ago. The first time I told anyone was in the 12th year. The person was a new friend, who didn't know how to deal with it and reacted harshly. Two years later, I selected two good friends and told them. I haven't regretted doing that. It's rare that I talk about feeling low with them; just knowing that they accept me as I am without judgement strengthens me.

So the trick is choosing the right person. It could be a family member, but it doesn't have to be. I was very selective in deciding who to tell. I'm all too aware of how complicated family relationships can be. There's nothing wrong with starting with someone who is not a relative, if you prefer.

When you're feeling low, anxious or worried, what you need is someone who is willing to listen, to empathise and, critically, to respond with compassion.

I speak to groups on mental health and well-being and this is one of the areas I include in all my talks – the benefits of having someone trustworthy to talk to. It took me years to open up with anyone I knew personally. But when I did, over time it became easier, and the benefits I experience are very much worth allowing myself to be vulnerable with someone else.

In general terms, I've found that engaging in stimulating conversation with others impacts me positively. I know that when you feel depressed, you're more inclined to retreat to your own private world. However, making the effort to phone someone, or strike up a chat with someone within reach, is often worth it. You can come away feeling re-energised and joyful.

This issue of identifying the right person is an important one, as it can be a sticking point for many people. It was for me.

One evening I was speaking at a men's event. During the Q&A, someone in the audience said many men would not feel comfortable talking to their friends or family if they felt depressed.

My advice was to speak to a professional. I did that myself. It's a very good place to start.

If the issue is ongoing, you might feel you need some more readily available, less formal, support; someone you can give a quick call or meet spontaneously for a drink or for a walk. That's when a family member or close friend can prove really helpful. They can provide you with a safe space to openly share your thoughts and talk things through.

I don't mean to labour the point, but making and maintaining those connections are critical to our resilience and well-being. There's a school of thought among people who write about depression from their personal experience of depression, that the condition is rooted in loss of human connections. Technological advancement is exciting, but can disrupt a sense of connectedness.

In the post-COVID world, this disconnect is set to grow and grow as we rely on technology like never before. During the lockdown period, I went for months without being touched. No hugs. No kisses. No handshakes. No reassuring pats on the back. No bumping into someone else. Nothing. I'm not an overly kinetic person, but I have friends who are very kinetic. I made the effort to reach out to them and say that I had called intentionally to acknowledge that, and ask how they were coping. To tell them I missed their hugs. It gave us cause to laugh and tease one another about our various idiosyncrasies.

In the 'new normal', as it's being called, we will all need to be more intentional about creating and maintaining our human connections. We will all need to be more intentional about caring for each other and meeting our emotional needs more deeply and effectively.

For years, particularly in the Western world, social isolation has been on the increase, with its mental and physical ill effects on individuals gaining attention even at governmental level. It is rife among older populations. Retirees who have lost their spouse and confidence to go out become increasingly housebound and cut off from the outside world. But the scourge of loneliness doesn't just affect older people; it's endemic among our youth and working-aged people too.

So how do we remain connected? How do we maintain our social skills? How can we maintain resilience and strengthen our emotional and mental well-being in a virtual world? I believe the answer is to be more intentional about it.

At another seminar I was asked, 'What can we do in general to support those we know who are depressed?'

One of the key things you can do is to make yourself available to them.

In my case, I chose a female friend and, more recently, a male friend who have made themselves available to me as my confidants in this journey. They became very close friends of mine very soon after I met them. I liked each of them because I could let my hair down and just relax when I was with either one. We laugh a lot together. We talk about serious things together. We push each other forward. We bounce ideas off each other. For me, in these relationships nobody is trying to change the other person. They're not trying to make me more like them and I'm not trying to make them more like me. There's no judgement. No criticism. No attempts, whether covertly or overtly, to reshape me in their image and likeness. With them, I am safe to do me and be me – and it's entirely reciprocal. I have actively established powerful and enduring connections with them both (incidentally, they don't know each other).

Over time, I decided to tell each of them about my depression. My instincts served me well, because that information did not alter their behaviour towards me or their perception of me. In fact, I rose in their estimation. They recognised that I truly was an overcomer who was fight a winning battle against a strong enemy.

I wasn't looking for pity or indulgence. I guess our connection had become so strong that I felt close to them, and it was such a wonderful feeling for me after years of feeling completely alone. It seemed right to confide in them about something that was such a big part of my life. Also, I just wanted my dear friends to know that there were times when I felt a crushing weight of joylessness, and didn't want to pretend to be OK. What kind of 'friend' is anyone who you have to put on a pretence with so they can accept you or be comfortable around you?

These two friends have made themselves available to me in the following ways:

- They do not judge;
- They allow me to be me;
- They listen and they respond with words of affirmation and compassion;
- They never dismiss or trivialise my concerns;
- They do not launch into offering solutions or try to 'fix' me;
- They do not tell me to 'snap out of it';
- They're not on some self-appointed mission to 'encourage' me;
- They haven't made depression a 'thing';
- They have not put me in a box with a label;
- They see me as I see myself – a resilient person.

These are some important attitudes to adopt if you want to relate with someone with this condition or who is feeling low in themselves. Another thing you can do is educate yourself about depression so you can better understand your loved one.

I consider these two friends to be superheroes. They mean so much to me. I have a great deal of respect for them both.

If your anxiety or low mood is persistent, it may mean that it is beyond the emotional highs and lows we all experience as part of life. You may need to seek a professional opinion. My advice is to book an appointment with your doctor.

Some people from particular cultures don't seem to trust their doctor or the medicines they are prescribed. I've had conversations with people seeking my reassurance that it's OK for them to take medicines prescribed by their doctor. Concerns are raised not only about anti-depressants, but medicines for physical illness as well. If you're of this persuasion, my advice is to have an open and honest conversation with your doctor. Ask them to explain why they've decided to prescribe a particular drug. What are its benefits, side effects, the length of time it would be safe for you to continue on them and the like? Share your concerns and doubts about anything that you are prescribed. Work with the doctor to find the best treatment for you. If your doctor is unwilling to have such a conversation, find another doctor.

The help I received from therapy was a game changer for me. My doctor referred me to a service that offered a range of therapy options. I choose to participate in Cognitive Behaviour Therapy (CBT), and continue to benefit from what I learned in those sessions.

As the lockdown continued, I heard more and more people expressing their frustration at being cooped up and wanting to return to going out freely, to meet with friends, shop, play sport, go to the gym and so on. At the same time, some people were concerned about the risks of resuming their lives outside their homes. It's quite an understandable mixture of feelings.

Whenever we come out of lockdown, we will be going back to places and using transport systems we haven't used in months. We will need to refamiliarise ourselves with the things we once took for granted. I'd say take it one step at a time, one day at a time. Talk about any fears, worries or anxieties you're feeling. Hear how friends and family are approaching it; see what works for you. Remember everyone is in the same boat. Take your time.

Remain informed of government guidance and information. Take whatever precautions you need to, to feel reassured about your safety as you go out and about.

I worked non-stop for four months during lockdown, from April to July, then realised I had run out of steam. This was despite working from home. You'd think working from home might not be as demanding as being in the office. To a large extent that is true. However, the daily grind of attending meeting after meeting online, having to meet deadlines and the like, never changed. I was in need of a break. So I took a week and went to a nice green venue in the East Midlands to recharge. It worked. If I had stayed home to 'rest' it would never have worked.

If you've been in your home over the last several months of the lockdown, it may be that you need a break. Before you make moves to readjust to venturing out again, it may well be worth going away from the home front for some days, if you can.

I was dubious at first. As I say, I'd been at home and enjoying being there. But that didn't stop me from eventually feeling quite weary psychologically. Working from home taxed me mentally. However, being away from home for a week made a huge difference; it really cleared my head and refreshed me. Upon my return to London, I was ready to go back to work again.

My break also gave me time to think about the way forward and prepare myself for it. It was a great way to set myself up for bouncing back.

27. EXERCISE THE POWER YOU DO HAVE

In life, we may think ourselves to be powerless, that we don't have a choice about how we live. But the reality is completely opposite. We are in fact powerful and can make choices to safeguard our mental and emotional health and well-being in any circumstance. You may be facing difficult challenges now and in the coming months related to employment, finances, relationships, health, but you do not have to be a passive recipient of whatever life throws your way. You can decide how you will manage yourself during the storms of life. Know that they will not last forever. Believe that you can and will find a way through to more stable times. Meanwhile, make your well-being a priority; use the strategies in this book. Get the help you need to solve the problems you face.

I would love to know how this book helped. Send me a message via twitter or Instagram @mshmjohnson

ACKNOWLEDGEMENTS

Thanks to all my family, relatives and friends for being in my life. I have the privilege of knowing some truly amazing human beings who I wish to also acknowledge. Their friendship plays an important role in my resilience and well-being.

- **Lyndon Wissart**; Chef and author of *The Inspired Diabetic*;
- **Njideka Meniru**; my sister-friend;
- **Dr Joan Myers OBE**; mentor and all-round inspirational figure.

Special thanks to **Tiffani Michelle Mapp**, who kindly agreed to write the foreword for *Bouncing Back*. Tiffani is a Psychology and Mental Health Services Professor and School Counsellor in Texas. She is also an International Neo-Soul Indie Artist Songwriter-Producer who goes by the name Taffani Michelle.

Aquila Farrell – thank you for being so inspiring and for your guidance on social media. **Simone Brown** – I'm grateful for our friendship. **Pat Issacs** – you're so faithful! **Chris Garcia** – you're amazing. God bless you **aunty Diane**. Thanks **Aunty Josie, Uncle James, Lyndon G** and **Lyndon E,** for taking some of the pressure off. **Shedley Branche** – thanks for riding in the ambulance; and with **Dex TheMac** and **Derrick McBurnette** breaking in the house – you guys are superheroes!

Conscious Dreams
PUBLISHING

Be the author of your own destiny

www.consciousdreamspublishing.com

info@consciousdreamspublishing.com

Let's connect

Lightning Source UK Ltd.
Milton Keynes UK
UKHW020632130921
390483UK00006B/48

9 781913 674601